G000066277

① Piazza del Campidoglio

Feel the glory of ancient Rome atop Capitoline _____ *Rome's seven hills. Here, conquering heroes dep*_____ _____ _____ _____ *principal shrine, the magnificent Temple of Jupiter. Completed in 509 BC, the temple was the site of the most sacred ceremonies, and from its lofty perch emperors enjoyed a bird's eye view of the arches and basilicas built in their honor. But, just as the Empire crumbled, so did this famous hilltop (by the Middle Ages, goats were grazing in the sacred ruins). Restoration began in 1537 when Pope Paul III asked Michelangelo to restore the site to its former splendor. The result — the picturesque **Piazza del Campidoglio** — is one of Rome's prettiest (and first) public piazzas. Three stately buildings occupy the square: the **Palazzo Senatorio** (Rome's City Hall), and the flanking **Palazzo Nuovo** and **Palazzo dei Conservatori** (which together house the Capitoline Museum; see annotation 2). At the piazza's center is a Michelangelo-designed pedestal, home to a replica of a statue of Emperor Marcus Aurelius (the original, dating to 161 AD, is in the Capitoline Museum). The piazza is reached by the operatic staircase known as the **Cordonata** (the only part of the project Michelangelo lived to see completed), and is guarded by the mythological marble twins, Castor and Pollux.*

Details: From Piazza Venezia, take steps to the right of the Vittorio Emanuele Monument.

② Capitoline Museum
Piazza del Campidoglio; Tel: 67102071

*Two majestic palazzos house the stunning antiquity collection of the Capitoline Museum, founded by Pope Sixtus IV in 1471 and enriched by four centuries of papal patronage. At **Palazzo Nuovo**, a compelling cast of marble characters awaits your inspection, led by the river god Marforio, who lazily lounges in his fountain while his bronze friend, Emperor Marcus Aurelius, gallantly gallops behind glass to the right. On the 2nd floor, the tragic 200 BC Dying Gaul merits a tearful visit (near entry staircase), before catching the sensual Capitoline Venus toweling off in the last room on the right. Take a peek at famous faces in history at the Hall of Philosophers (with busts of chief thinkers like Homer and Cicero) and the Hall of Emperors (65 marble heads show off the latest imperial hairdos; last rooms on left on 2nd floor). In the stunning **Palazzo dei Conservatori**, don't miss the enormous body parts from Constantine's colossal statue (in the courtyard) that once stood in the Roman Forum, and the 6th-century BC Capitoline Wolf (the symbol of Rome). To the right of Palazzo Nuovo, take in a great **view** of the Roman Forum off Via San Pietro in Carcere.*

Details: Tues. to Sat., 9-7, Sun., 9-7. Last entry 30 minutes before closing. Cost: LL.

③ Santa Maria in Aracoeli
Piazza d'Aracoeli; Tel: 6798155

Sharing real estate on the Piazza del Campidoglio is this charming church — a highly revered spot in ancient Rome when the Temple of Juno <u>Moneta</u> housed the Roman Mint on this site (hence the derivation of the word "money"). The present church dates to 1250 and was the political center of medieval Rome, and the setting for fiery speeches by Roman leaders. Church highlights include: 22 interior columns taken from the Forum's ancient buildings, ceiling decorations commemorating the Battle of Lepanto of 1571 (when the Christian army defeated the Turks), and 15th-century frescoes of St. Bernard of Siena by Pinturicchio (first chapel on right). The truly pious reach the church by climbing its steep 122 marble steps on their knees (the quicker route is via a staircase found to the right of Palazzo Nuovo).

Details: Mon. to Sat., 7 am-8 pm, Sun., 9-10:30, 12-5.

Forum of Caesar
Off Via dei Fori Imperiali

Julius Caesar built the first of Rome's five Imperial Forums ("public squares") in 46 BC to ease congestion when the original Roman Forum could no longer serve the rapidly growing population. Caesar's motives, however, were less than pure — he wanted a major landmark to celebrate his spectacular rise to power (Caesar declared himself dictator in 44 BC only to be assassinated that same year, putting an end to his unbridled ambition and sparking a 17-year civil war; when the dust settled, Rome, once a Republic, was governed by emperors). Caesar spared no expense in building his legacy, leveling the private houses that stood in his way and creating a rectangular area of shops, statues and essential tributes. Soon, emperors from Augustus to Trajan followed suit, adding their own glorious monuments to the Roman landscape (see annotations 5 to 7). The result: five interconnected forums where citizens could conduct their commercial, political and legal affairs while paying homage to imperial accomplishments. The primary remains of Caesar's Forum are three columns from the Temple of Venus and Genetrix (which once housed statues of Venus, Cleopatra and, of course, Caesar himself).

Details: Viewed any time. Reached by Via San Pietro in Carcere (left of Palazzo Senatorio).

Forum of Trajan
Between Via dei Fori Imperiali and Via Alessandrina

*Imperial one-upmanship reached its pinnacle under Emperor Trajan, who completed the last (and largest) of the five Imperial Forums in 115 AD. His vast complex of libraries, market halls, gardens and colonnades — capped by Basilica Ulpia (the largest covered hall ever built in Rome) — left visiting rulers speechless. The Forum's two most visible survivors are **Trajan's Market** (see annotation 6) and **Trajan's Column**, one of the ancient world's great architectural achievements (preserved wholly intact courtesy of the death penalty imposed by the Roman Senate upon anyone who mutilated it). Inaugurated in 113 AD, the 130-foot marble column is a sculpted newsreel of Trajan's successful campaign over the Dacians. The reliefs, depicting over 2,500 figures, are some of the western world's most intricate (sparking poor copycats throughout Europe). A statue of Trajan once stood at its top (replaced by St. Peter in 1587). Though binoculars are your best bet for viewing this marvel today, in Trajan's time Roman citizens perused the carvings from roof terraces of Greek and Latin libraries next door.*

Details: Viewed any time.

Trajan's Market
Via IV Novembre at Via Magnanapoli; Tel: 6790048

Fans of Macy's, Harrods and Bloomingdale's have Emperor Trajan to thank for creating the world's first department store in 112 AD! Conjure up the noises, smells and colors of ancient Rome as you weave through these impressive semi-circular, red-bricked remains, once the hub of the Roman food supply network. Over 150 shopkeepers operated out of "tabernae" (single room, barrel-vaulted units), selling the latest Roman hors d'oeuvres. The tabernae were arranged in levels, and each floor specialized in a given product (wine on first, spices on third, fish on fifth ... sound familiar?). The market, whose appearance today looks much the same as it did in Trajan's day, was covered over in medieval times and not unearthed until 1924. A small museum inside shows remains from excavations conducted on site.

Details: Tues. to Sat., 9-7, Sun., 9-1. Last entry one hour before closing. Cost: L.

Forum of Augustus
Via Alessandrina

*Augustus, Caesar's adopted son, took over the reigns of power after his father's assassination, becoming Rome's first emperor and ruling from 27 BC to 14 AD. He presided over the golden age of the Roman Empire, establishing lasting peace, initiating economic reform and constructing scores of marble monuments. Augustus's building spree culminated in this landmark, the second of the Imperial Forums, dedicated in 2 BC. Today, its principal remains are 17 steps (and some broken columns) from the Temple of Mars the Avenger, built to commemorate Augustus's victory at Philippi over his father's assassins, Brutus and Cassius (Caesar's sword and other treasures were kept on display at the temple). The firewall in the back — the outline of which can still be imagined — protected the Forum from the arson-prone residents of the adjacent Suburra district (the haunt of thieves and murderers). Underneath Via dei Fori Imperiali are two other Imperial Forums (currently undergoing excavation): the **Forum of Vespasian**, completed in 70 AD, and the **Forum of Nerva**, completed in 97 AD.*

Details: Viewed any time (sketch to left of site shows the Forum's original appearance).

 San Pietro in Vincoli
Entrance at Via San Francesco di Paola, off Via Cavour; Tel: 4882865

Built to house the chains ("vincoli") which bound St. Peter when he was a prisoner in Jerusalem, San Pietro in Vincoli has long been a popular stop among the faithful. But the church's popularity grew even greater when it became home to one of Michelangelo's most well-known sculptures, the **Moses**. *The artist — who often boasted that he "drank in the chisel and hammer with his mother's milk" (his wet nurse was a stone-carver's wife!) — captures Moses at the moment he brought* The Ten Commandments *down from Mt. Sinai. The work was originally intended to be one of 40 statues that formed an elaborate final resting place for Pope Julius II, who commissioned the piece in 1505. But the demands of the Sistine Chapel — and the desire of Julius's successor, Pope Paul III, who preferred that Michelangelo finish* The Last Judgment *— ensured that the project would not be completed. Ultimately, Pope Julius's remains were shoveled into an unmarked grave in St. Peter's, and Moses was placed here (and surrounded by the work of other sculptors).*

Details: Mon. to Sat., 7-12:30, 3:30-6, Sun., 7-12.

 Roman Forum (see map on back cover)
Enter on Via dei Fori Imperiali; Tel: 6990110

Conjure up the days when togas were in vogue at this field of ruins, once the heart of all commercial, judicial and political life in ancient Rome. The Roman Forum got its start in 750 BC as a patch of swampy land set in a valley below Rome's seven hills. Settlers gathered in this common "meeting ground" to barter and gossip … and from these small beginnings grew a five-acre public area filled with temples, arches, law courts, markets and more. Here, "bankers and brokers, bakers and butchers …" participated in elections, funerals, sacrifices and celebrations (Caesar hosted a torchlit banquet for 22,000!). The Forum operated as the center of public life until 46 BC, when Caesar decided to build his own, a practice emulated by several subsequent emperors (see annotations 4 to 7). In the 5th century, the Forum suffered extensive damage when the city was sacked by barbarians. By the Middle Ages, the area was a cow pasture, and it was not until the 19th century that the ruins were excavated.

Today, ancient Rome's most famous buildings can be brought to life with a little imagination. Strolling counterclockwise from the entrance, Forum highlights are: **Basilica Aemilia** *(built in 179 BC as a meeting place for money changers, whose copper coins are still fused into the* *pavement in front of these very meager ruins);* **Curia** *(this red brick home of the Roman Senate is a 20th-century restoration of the one Emperor Diocletian built in 283 AD);* **Arch of Septimius Severus** *(built in 203 AD to celebrate Emperor Septimius Severus's victory over the Parthians; note the top inscription which once honored Septimius and his sons, Caracalla and Geta; when Caracalla murdered his brother he also had his name removed);* **Rostra** *(the platform where "friends, Romans and countrymen" gathered to hear the great public figures of ancient Rome make many a famous speech);* **Temple of Saturn** *(eight graceful Ionic columns are all that remain of one of Rome's oldest temples, built in 497 BC and once home to the state treasury);* **Basilica Giulia** *(created by Caesar in 54 BC to serve as the central law courts; only foundations and statue pedestals stand from this football-field-sized landmark, as do "gaming boards" scratched into the front pavement — no doubt the work of those awaiting the outcome of trials);* **Temple of Castor and Pollux** *(three lone columns mark the 5th-century BC temple where magistrates were sworn in);* **Temple of Caesar** *(whose altar marks the spot of Caesar's cremation);* **Temple of Vesta** *(a half circle of columns indicates the tiny temple where special priestesses, known as Vestal Virgins, tended Rome's "sacred flame"; the Vestals were chosen between ages 6 and 10 and required to remain chaste for 30 years — Vestals that didn't live by the rules were buried alive, those that did received preferential treatment at all events, including the best seats at the Colosseum);* **House of the Vestal Virgins** *(where the Vestals lived; only the courtyard remains, surrounded by crumbling statues of members of the Order);* **Arch of Titus** *(built in 81 AD to celebrate Titus's conquest of Jerusalem, an event commemorated in its two inside reliefs; during the Middle Ages, no Jew would pass under the arch);* **Via Sacra** *(the main thoroughfare along which victorious emperors would parade wagonloads of loot from their latest conquest; the outlines of the road can still be seen);* **Antiquarium Forense** *(with excavated finds from the Forum; Mon. to Sat., 9-5, Sun., 9-1);* **Basilica of Maxentius and Constantine** *(dating to 308 AD and used for judicial hearings, it was one of Rome's largest buildings, and so impressive that Bramante studied it in his design for St. Peter's; three huge coffered vaults remain); and* **Temple of Antoninus and Faustina** *(built in 141 AD; the columns survived in fairly good condition because a church was built inside it in the Middle Ages).*

Details: Mon. to Sat., 9-5 (may close later in summer; closes at 4 in Nov., Dec. and Jan.), Sun., 9-2. Last entry one hour before closing. Cost: Free.

⑩ **Palatine Hill**
Enter near Arch of Titus in Forum or on Via San Gregorio; Tel: 6990110

The word "palace" is derived from this very hill — once the home of emperors and now a tranquil jumble of ancient hilltop ruins. The city's most famous inhabitants built residences here, starting with Romulus (Rome's first king) and Augustus (Rome's first emperor). Infamous rulers like Caligula and Nero also enjoyed the cool breezes that wafted over the hilltop, but it was Emperor Domitian (81-96 AD) who made the Palatine the ancient equivalent of Buckingham Palace, building a sumptuous mansion used by successors until 305 AD (this colossal edifice once ranked "among the most beautiful things in the world"). Poorly marked ruins now dominate the hill but, with some perseverance, you may be able to find the following (approach from Arch of Titus entrance along Clivo Palatino): **Farnese Gardens** *(lavish private botanical gardens built by the Farneses in the 16th century and most noted for a great overall* **view** *of the Forum from the terrace; uphill on your right);* **Domus Flavia** *(once the public rooms of Domitian's incredible palace; the very scanty ruins include fragments of beautiful tiled dining room floors; just south of gardens);* **Domus Augustana** *(Domitian's private digs and a place he rarely left for fear of assassins; to no avail as he was killed in his bedroom; ruins are marked by an upper and lower level courtyard);* **Domitian's Stadium** *(used for private horse races; the shape and walls can still be seen), and the* **House of Livia** *(where Augustus lived with his wife Livia from 38 BC to his death in 14 AD; the modest house still* contains parts of mythological frescoes that adorned the reception rooms; reached by doubling back towards the Arch of Titus entrance).

Details: Mon. to Sat., 9-5 (may close later in summer; closes at 4 in Nov., Dec. and Jan.), Sun., 9-2. Last entry one hour before closing. Cost: LLL.

11 Arch of Constantine
Between Via San Gregorio and Piazza del Colosseo

Religious significance and architectural inventiveness clash at the Arch of Constantine, built in 315 AD to celebrate Emperor Constantine's victory over rival (and co-Emperor) Maxentius. One of ancient Rome's most controversial landmarks, the arch represents a political comprise: the dedication to "Instinctus Divinatus" (note the top inscription) signaled Constantine's belief in Christianity (a shunned religion until Constantine became its powerful patron), yet satisfied pagan Senators who didn't want to put Christ's name on a public monument. Unfortunately, Christian principles didn't extend to the arch's design — Constantine pillaged other landmarks throughout Rome, lifting sculptures to earlier emperors and replacing their heads with his own (leading the great Renaissance artist Raphael to call the arch "stupid and ridiculous"). To the north are the excavated foundations of **Meta Sudans** ("Sweating Point"), a colossal fountain dating to 80 AD, named for the marker around which chariots turned during races.

Details: Viewed any time.

12 Colosseum
Piazza del Colosseo; Tel: 7004261

No visit to Rome is complete without a trip to "that noble wreck in ruinous perfection" — the Colosseum. In this prototype for every modern sports stadium, ancient Rome would be entertained daily with a rotating assortment of violent gladiator contests, chariot fights, mock naval battles and wild beast shows (thousands of animals would emerge from cells beneath the arena, only to be slashed and slaughtered by "beast slayers"). Emperors drew power and prestige from the shows they offered the masses, and the more blood spewed, the more the crowd loved it. Emperor Vespasian started construction of the Colosseum in 72 AD over the lake that stood in the gardens of Nero's vast palace. Eight years later, Vespasian's son, Titus, "threw out the first ball," opening this sporting arena in a 100-day celebration involving 5,000 slaughtered beasts. Over 50,000 spectators could take in the blood orgies, entering through 76 gates numbered to correspond to seat locations (the lower your seat, the higher your social status). "State-of-the-art" features included: rope-pulled elevators (to bring up gladiators and animals from tunnels beneath the wooden floor; the intricate passages are readily viewable); a flooding system (to fill the stadium floor with water for mock naval battles); an adjustable awning operated by sailors (to cover the arena in bad weather); and vomitoria (quick exits available for spectators who gorged on too many Roman hot dogs!). By the 5th century, the arena's allure faded and ultimately it was turned into a quarry (which explains the Colosseum's current Swiss-cheese look). Visit the upper floor to get the full effect!

Details: Mon. to Sat., 9-5 (may close later in summer; closes at 4 in Nov., Dec. and Jan.), Sun., 9-2. Cost: LL.

13 Clivo di Scauro
Contemplate early Christian Rome along this cobbled "country lane" — a detour definitely worth making on your way from the Colosseum to the Circus Maximus. Begin your heavenly ascent at **San Gregorio Magno**, a pretty church incorporated into the remains of Pope

*Gregory the Great's 6th-century monastery. Monks still live on site, offering natural products for sale in the shop to the right of the church (Piazza di San Gregorio; daily, 9:30-12, 3:30-6). A short wander uphill leads to **Santi Giovanni e Paolo**, begun in the 4th century (though rebuilt several times since) and one of the earliest Christian meeting places in the city. The interior dates to the 18th century, and its huge chandeliers and painted walls lend it an air more appropriate to a luxurious palazzo than a place of worship (Sat. to Thurs., 9-11:30, 4-6). A couple of yards further up, on your right, a small door serves as an entrance to the **park of Villa Celimontana**, a hidden slice of Eden. In the once vast vineyards of the 16th-century Mattei family retreat, natives come to stroll in a stunning tree-covered landscape. Finally, check out **Antiquarium Romano**, home to a valuable collection of Greek and Roman antiquities (Viale Parco del Celio; Tues. to Sat., 10-4, Sun., 10-1; Cost: LL).*

Details: Accessed by steps on the eastern side of Via San Gregorio (steps are marked "Antiquarium Romano").

14 Circus Maximus
Between Via dei Cerchi and Via del Circo Massimo

"A day at the races" in ancient Rome was not your average trip to Ascot! Only a large grassy oval occupies the site of what was once Rome's favorite racetrack, where 250,000+ Romans, sitting on marble bleachers, cheered on their most beloved charioteers! Built by King Tarquinius Priscus in the 7th-century BC, the Circus Maximus was enlarged under Caesar in 46 BC and rebuilt several times after that. In its heyday, citizens could wager on up to 24 chariot races a day, taking their winnings to the taverns and brothels located in the arches under the seats. The attendant pomp and circumstance was almost as entertaining as the races — a drop of a white hankie signaled a procession of clowns, trick riders and chariots (drawn by two to ten jewel-bedecked horses). The charioteers would do seven laps, careening around the obelisk-laden spine in a cloud of dust. The Circus Maximus was closed in the 6th century and later scavenged for building materials. Today, only a strong ear may pick up the ghostly rumble of horse hooves, and the site is best for strollers and joggers.

Details: Viewed any time.

15 Santa Maria in Cosmedin
Piazza della Bocca della Verità 18; Tel: 6781419

*Medieval Rome's version of "truth or dare" is represented by the oversized drain cover in this church's courtyard. Shaped in the form of a stone face, the cover (a.k.a. "the Mouth of Truth") allegedly dispensed justice by biting the hand of a liar (or so the story goes anyway). Today, the only hands in the mouth are those attached to tourists who find it the ultimate photo op! The church — whose highlights include an intricate mosaic floor and a frescoed frieze — dates to the 6th century, and its bell tower (Rome's tallest) was added in the 12th century. In earlier times, Rome's famous cattle market (the Forum Boarium) operated here, and as far back as the 5th century BC boats floated up the Tiber laden with bovine bounty. Ancient remnants litter the area including, in the church's piazza, two small, 2nd-century BC temples: the round **Temple of Vesta** (misnamed, and actually dedicated to Hercules, the patron of the Forum Boarium), and the square **Temple of Fortuna Virilis** (dedicated to the god of ports). Around the corner, on Via Velabro, the 4th-century **Arch of Janus** marked the northern entrance to the Forum Boarium (merchants conducted their business in the shade of the arch).*

Details: Daily, 9-12, 3-5.

Teatro di Marcello/Portico d'Ottavia
Via Teatro di Marcello/Via Portico d'Ottavia

Nicknamed the "baby Colosseum" for the raucous, often violent, performances staged to packed houses of 20,000, the 11 BC **Teatro di Marcello** *is one of the few remnants of ancient Rome's Campus Martius (bounded by the Tiber and today's Via del Corso). The Campus Martius was a vast open field, initially a military training ground, that became, by 27 BC, a sparsely inhabited home to theatres, baths, pleasure grounds, shaded gardens and assorted monuments. But, when the barbarians stopped up the Roman water supply, the population was forced to move closer to the Tiber and most of the Campus Martius facilities were destroyed. The Teatro was ultimately converted to a fortress, then a Renaissance palazzo and, today, it is an upscale condo (and the world's oldest continuously inhabited building). To its west, and dating to 149 BC, is* **Portico d'Ottavia** *— once the entrance to a massive colonnaded complex of libraries and temples, and now shelter to the church of Sant'Angelo in Pescheria (named for the fish market held here in the Middle Ages).*

Details: Viewed any time.

 ### Picture-Perfect Piazzas

Let the sound of trickling water lure you to three enchanting piazzas clustered near Teatro di Marcello. Though almost all of Rome's piazzas have **fountains** *(many fed by aqueducts the Romans built in the 2nd century BC to provide the city with an adequate water supply), our favorite is the* **Piazza Mattei**'s *Fontana delle Tartarughe, built by Florentine sculptor Taddeo Landini in 1585. Four naked boys lift bronze tortoises into the fountain in a graceful and elegant pose. Overlooking the piazza are remnants of 16th-century palazzos built by the wealthy Mattei family, who settled here after they were ousted from the Trastevere district for one too many murders. Just south,* **Piazza Campitelli** *is one of the most romantic corners of Rome, anchored by a charming fountain and the church of Santa Maria in Campitelli, a 17th-century "thank-you" from grateful Roman citizens happy that an outbreak of the plague was over (daily, 7-12, 4-7). And to the north, lovely* **Piazza Margana** *is a tiny treasure of vine-covered ochre and yellow 16th-century buildings.*

Details: Viewed any time.

 ### The Jewish Ghetto

The longest surviving Jewish community in the western world can be found in this small, mazelike area known as Rome's Jewish Ghetto (approximately bounded by Via Portico d'Ottavia, Lungotevere dei Cenci and Via Arenula). Seeds of the Jewish community were sown in 159 BC when residents of Judea were sent to Rome to establish a community as part of a diplomatic mission; they set up camp in nearby Trastevere (see annotation 61). The harmonious relationship lasted until 1555, when Pope Paul IV sequestered the 3,500+ Roman Jews in this cramped neighborhood, building a wall and locking the gates at night. Though the walls were torn down in 1848, a quarter of the ghetto's Jews were deported to concentration camps during World War II. The neighborhood still caters to the city's Jewish population, and a stroll on Via Portico d'Ottavia takes you past a number of kosher bakeries and restaurants. The **synagogue** *— at Tiber's edge — contains a* **museum** *chronicling the history of the Roman Jewish experience with ceremonial objects, scrolls, torah finials and maps of the ghetto (Lungotevere dei Cenci 15).*

Details: Synagogue: guided tours Mon. to Thurs., 9:30-1:30, 2-4, Fri., 9:30-2, Sun., 9:30-12:30. Cost: LL.

19 Palazzo Spada
Piazza Capo di Ferro 3; Tel: 6861158

*Glorious stuccoed figures of renowned Romans welcome you to this masterful 16th-century palazzo, one of the most distinctive of Rome's Renaissance mansions. Cardinal Spada, papal legate to Bologna, acquired the palazzo in 1632 and hired the great architect Borromini to add a decorative flourish. Borromini's triumph is the colonnaded gallery off the courtyard (to the left of entrance). Peer down a "mile-long" hall of Doric columns to a "colossal" statue — in reality, the corridor is only 15 feet and the statue pygmy-sized! Today, the palazzo houses the Council of State, but its second floor **gallery** is open to the public and contains four rooms filled with Cardinal Spada's private art collection of choice 15th to 18th-century paintings. A short hop west leads to **Palazzo Farnese**, commissioned by Alexander Farnese in 1534 to the designs of da Sangallo, della Porta and Michelangelo, and so lavish that its construction almost bankrupted the powerful Farneses. The palazzo is now home to the French Embassy (closed to public), and its **piazza** is the site of two fountains made from tubs taken from the Baths of Caracalla. Allegedly, the tubs were moved here in the 16th century when bull baiting ceremonies were held in the piazza (the baiters jumped into the tubs for protection!).*

Details: Tues. to Sat., 9–7, Sun., 9-1. Last entry 30 minutes before closing. Cost: LL.

20 Campo de' Fiori

*The specialties of the Roman table — from prosciutto to parmesan — can be found at this colorful open-air market located in a pretty, cobbled square in the heart of "old Rome." The area, however, did not always dish up gastronomic treasures — in fact, a "field of flowers" (campo de' fiori) blanketed the site until the 15th century, when major palazzos were built nearby and this neighborhood became a bustling metropolis of inns and crafts shops catering to aristocrats. In the 16th century, the Campo took on a more ominous tone when public executions took place in its square, most notably that of philosopher Giordano Bruno, who was burned at the stake in 1600 for heresy (his hooded statue marks the spot of his death). Detour west into the ancient side streets **Via Cappellari** and **Via del Pellegrino**, now a charming cluster of artisans and antique dealers. North of the Campo is handsome **Palazzo della Cancelleria**, built in 1485 by Cardinal Raffaele Riario and financed with the proceeds from one night's gambling earnings. In 1518, Riario tried to poison Pope Leo X and the building was confiscated and turned into the papal chancellery (open only for occasional evening concerts).*

Details: Market: Mon. to Sat., 7-1.

21 Via Giulia

*Whether or not you are one of the fortunate few who can make a purchase at the elegant **antique shops** lining this stately thoroughfare, a stroll down Via Giulia is an absolute must! Bramante laid out this cobbled street in 1508 at the behest of Pope Julius II (hence "Giulia") to give pilgrims easier Vatican access. By the mid 16th-century, the street was a prime address for Vatican movers and shakers, many of whose elegant mansions still stand, beginning with **Palazzo Farnese** (see annotation 19; whose backyard anchors Via Giulia's east end; note Michelangelo's ivy-covered archway, built in a failed attempt to link the Farnese family's two retreats, Palazzo Farnese and Villa Farnesina). Noteworthy street sights include: **Palazzo Falconieri** (with sculpted falcons adorning its facade, and courtyard by Borromini; Via Giulia 1); **Santa Maria dell'Orazione e Morte** (once dedicated to the burial of the poor, skulls decorate its door; intersection of Via dei Farnese); **Oratorio del Gonfalone** (built in the 16th-century by the Flag-Bearers Guild; open for evening concerts; Vic. d. Scimia; tel: 6875952); **Palazzo Sacchetti** (the 16th-century home of architect da Sangallo the*

*Younger; Via Giulia 66 at Vic. Cefalo); and glorious **San Giovanni dei Fiorentini** (begun in 1614 to cater to the Florentine community; over a century in the making, the church is laden with masterworks of Tuscan artists, including Borromini, who designed the high altar and is buried in front of it; Mon. to Sat., 7-12, 4:30-7, Sun., 7:30-1, 5-7:30).*

Details: For store hours see "Shopping" on the Helpful Hints page. Most of the palazzos aren't open to the public, but you can sneak a peek into the courtyards.

Vatican City (also see annotations 23 to 25)

The world's smallest state, Vatican City packs an awfully large historical punch! This is the seat of the Pope, leader of the Catholic world, who dates his authority to when Jesus sent Peter to Rome to preach the gospel. The Pope presides over 109 acres of the most sacred shrines of Christiandom, including St. Peter's and the Vatican Palace (the papal residence since 1377, and now home to the rarest of artworks). A sovereign state since the signing of the Lateran Treaty in 1929, the Vatican operates under its own laws, and has its own national anthem, newspaper, radio station, post office and police force (known as the Swiss Guards). The Pope, who governs Vatican City in addition to his spiritual duties, is selected by a conclave of the College of Cardinals, voting by secret ballot under Michelangelo's frescoes in the Sistine Chapel (when all the votes are in, white smoke emanates from a chimney above St. Peter's signaling the new pope's election – black smoke indicates no majority has been reached).

Details: See annotations 23 to 25 for details.

Piazza San Pietro (St. Peter's Square)

*Gian Lorenzo Bernini (1598-1680) left his stamp on churches and monuments throughout Rome, but his deepest impression can be found in the sweeping entry courtyard to St. Peter's. Laid out between 1656 and 1667, Bernini's curving-arm design symbolizes "an open embrace to the world" – and from the sheer size of the piazza, it looks as if the world could fit into it (max: 400,000)! The piazza is decorated with 284 columns, topped by 140 statues of saints, and at its center is the Vatican **obelisk** which once stood at Nero's Circus where early Christian martyrs were slaughtered. The ball on the summit contains pieces of the Holy Cross, inserted when Pope Sixtus V had the 500-ton obelisk moved here in 1586 from a spot just south of the basilica (a major engineering feat, requiring the services of 900 men and 140 horses). The building beyond the right colonnade is where the present Pope lives and works, and on Sun. at noon he appears in his study window to **bless** those gathered in the piazza. On the piazza's left side is the **Vatican Tourist Office** from which you can get maps, reserve **garden tours** (two hour tour: Mar. to Oct., Mon., Tues., Thurs., Fri., Sat. at 10; Nov. to Feb., Sat. at 10; Cost: LLL; book tour in advance) and take the **bus** to the entrance of the Vatican Museums (tourist office: Mon. to Sat., 8:30-7; tel: 69884466; fax: 69885100).*

Details: Papal Audiences: see Helpful Hints page.

St. Peter's
Piazza San Pietro; Tel: 69884466

St. Peter's, the massive basilica dedicated to the Apostle Peter (Jesus's aide and the first Pope), is a Guinness Book of Records favorite – it is the world's largest church, topped by the world's largest dome and decorated with some of the world's greatest art. Emperor Constantine built a basilica here in 324 AD over the alleged tomb of St. Peter, naming it "the head of all churches of the world" (Constantine's conversion to Christianity in 314 AD gave the once-shunned religion the official stamp of approval). By mid 15th-century, Old St. Peter's was starting to show its age and, in 1506, Pope Julius II laid the foundation stone for a new church, hiring architectural genius Donato Bramante for the design. The construction of St. Peter's outlasted Julius and Bramante, as well as successors Raphael, Peruzzi, da Sangallo, and others. Overall credit is generally given to 72-year old Michelangelo, chief architect from 1547 to his death in 1564, who designed much of the present structure, most notably the celebrated 435-foot dome (though Michelangelo died before its completion).

Inside, keeping company with the tombs of popes and saints, are masterpieces worthy of any major museum. Highlights include (working counterclockwise): Michelangelo's famous Pietà (finished in 1498 when he was 24 and the only sculpture he ever signed, allegedly because he overheard the finished work attributed to a second rate artist; first chapel on right, behind glass); Bernini's bronze Baldacchino (cast in 1633, the canopy of twisting bronze columns shelters the Pope when he conducts mass; under dome); di Cambio's 13th-century Statue of St. Peter (whose right foot has been polished by the kisses of thousands of pilgrims; right pillar in front of Baldacchino); Bernini's Throne of St. Peter (completed in 1666 to enclose the remains of St. Peter's wooden episcopal chair; apse); and Bernini's Tomb of Pope Alexander VII (with figures of Truth, Justice, Charity and Prudence to keep Alexander company in the after-life; left chapel after transept). Head up to the **dome's top** *for amazing views of Rome (be prepared for long lines and 330 steep steps), or descend into the* **grottoes** *to see a panoply of papal tombs. Best of all, take a guided tour of the underground* **necropolis***, a 1st-century cemetery containing the tomb of St. Peter himself.*

Details: Basilica: Daily, 7-7 (to 6 from Oct.-Mar.). Cost: Free. Dome: Daily, 8-6 (to 5 from Oct.-Mar.). Elevator goes to interior level, then it's a very strenuous climb up 330 steps to an outdoor gallery. Cost: LL. Grottoes: Daily, 7-6 (to 5 from Oct.-Mar.). Cost: Free. Necropolis: via 90-minute guided tour only, daily, 9-5; reserve in advance at Uffizio degli Scavi, to left of church entrance where Swiss Guard is stationed (tel: 69885318). Cost: LLL. You are not allowed inside the church in shorts, short skirts or sleeveless blouses.

 ### Vatican Museums
Enter at Viale Vaticano; Tel: 69883333

If only the Vatican Palace could talk, what papal privileges it would reveal! Centuries of history are etched into these walls, the official residence of the popes since 1377. Borne from two 5th-century villas near St. Peter's, today's luxurious complex is primarily the work of the Renaissance popes — Pope Nicholas V (1447-1455) to Pope Paul III (1534-1549) — who built the papal seat into the jewel it is today (these promoters of the arts were also the most corrupt popes ever to hold the office!). Visitors can wander among the suites of past popes and tour numerous separate museums (collectively known as the Vatican Museums). A visit to this huge complex can be daunting, and you should follow one of the Vatican's **four suggested itineraries** *(A, B, C, D), ranging in scope from 1.5 to 5 hours. Highlights are:*

Pio-Clementine Museum *(itineraries C and D only): This museum houses the sculptural superstars of the ancient Roman and Greek worlds. Don't leave Rome without a view of the haunting 1st-century AD Laocoön (who, with his two sons, strains against the deathly hug of a serpent sent by Apollo's priest), and the muscular 1st-century BC Belvedere Torso (which inspired Michelangelo in the nudes he painted in the Sistine Chapel).*

Galleries of Candelabra, Tapestries and Maps *(all itineraries): Massive halls divide you from your goal of reaching the Sistine Chapel, and though their lengths can be daunting, their decor is dynamite. Take in the Gallery of the Candelabra (whose 2,000 year old candlesticks give the gallery its name), Gallery of Tapestries (with 16th-century tapestries designed by disciples of Raphael depicting the life of Christ), and our favorite, the 400-foot Gallery of Maps (an impressive cartographic display of 40 maps of Italy, painted by Ignazio Danti in 1580).*

Raphael Rooms (itineraries C and D only): Pope Julius II commissioned Renaissance artist Raphael to decorate this suite of rooms in 1508, destroying the work of earlier masters to make room for the designs of his young protege. Painted by Raphael and his assistants between 1508 and 1524, the rooms served as the official apartments of 11 popes – from Julius II (1503-1513) to Gregory XIII (1572-1585) – and contain some of the world's greatest thematic paintings. The four rooms are: the Stanza di Constantino (Room 1; papal reception hall; decorated with scenes from the life of Constantine; painted after Raphael's death); the Stanza d'Eliodoro (Room 2; papal antechamber; showing events in the history of the church); the Stanza della Segnatura (Room 3; papal library, whose celebrated fresco, The School of Athens, shows famous philosophers with the faces of Raphael's contemporaries – note Michelangelo in the guise of Hericlitus, leaning on a stone in the lower portion), and the Stanza dell'Incendio (Room 4; papal dining room; showing scenes in the lives of Popes Leo III and IV; painted to Raphael's design by his assistants).

Sistine Chapel (all itineraries): Pope Julius II commissioned Michelangelo to paint the Sistine Chapel ceiling in 1508, a project the artist would later regret. He wrote: "I live in great toil and weariness of body. I have no friends and don't want any…" No wonder Michelangelo was complaining – for five long years (1508-1512) he stood on a dizzying scaffold seven stories high, staring up at a 3,000 square foot blank space while Pope Julius took him to task for not working fast enough (upon completion, the artist could read only by holding books above his head!). But Michelangelo's personal pain resulted in the world's finest artistic legacy – nine monumental ceiling panels tell the story of Genesis from Creation to the Flood. Images of prophets surround the scenes, and triangular spandrels depict Christ's ancestors. Michelangelo made 200 preliminary drawings, ultimately using full sized cartoons which he traced by pin dots into the ceiling.

Twenty five years later, Michelangelo reluctantly returned to paint **The Last Judgment**, which depicts 300 souls swirling around Christ the Judge (behind you as you enter the chapel). Painting from 1536 to 1541, Michelangelo was in a more pessimistic frame of mind, apparent from the harsher features of the figures (undoubtedly a reflection of his Sistine Chapel experience which he deemed "a punishment by God"). When The Last Judgment was unveiled, Pope Paul III was so overcome that he fell to his knees in prayer (the Pope's successors didn't love the art quite as much, and Pope Pius IV covered up some of the nudes with loincloths in 1564!). Frequently overlooked by neck-craning visitors are the side walls, lined with frescoed scenes from the lives of Moses and Christ, and painted by superstars like Botticelli and Signorelli. Closed for a 14-year restoration, the chapel reopened in 1994.

Vatican Library (various parts are covered on all itineraries): In 1447, Pope Nicholas V started the earth's richest library with 340 volumes. Successive Popes deposited their favorite editions into this 16th-century addition, decorating numerous galleries to house them all. The decor reaches its peak in the Great Hall, loaded with frescoes of major papal events.

Pinacoteca (itineraries B and D only): Da Vinci, Caravaggio, Raphael and company will entertain you with masterpieces that would normally create lines three-deep were it not for the competition at the nearby Sistine Chapel. Most lose their steam by the time they reach this picture gallery, but the persistent are well-rewarded!

Details: Mid Mar.-mid June and Sept. 1-end Oct., Mon. to Fri., 8:45-4, Sat., 8:45-1:45; Rest of year, Mon. to Sat., 8:45-1:45. Also open last Sun. of each month, 8:45-1:45 (free entry on Sun.). Last entry 45 minutes before closing. Cost: LLL. To avoid massive lines, arrive at 8 when museums are open to 1:45, and noon when museums are open to 4:45. Bring binoculars to best view Sistine Chapel ceiling.

26 **The Borgo**

In medieval times, this small neighborhood catered to the pilgrims that came to town with a selection of churches, monasteries and hostelries. Today, the Borgo still serves Vatican visitors, with tourist shops lining the main thoroughfare of Via della Conciliazone (created by Mussolini when he cut a swath through the area's alleys in 1936) and particularly good trattorias tucked on the less-trafficked side streets. As you make your way through the Borgo, note the high **rampart** running along Via dei Corrodori – a constant reminder that, in turbulent times, the popes could make a quick exit from the Vatican to Castel Sant'Angelo, as Clement VII did in 1527 when Charles V sacked Rome (the Pope's white robes visible from the streets below).

Details: Viewed any time.

(27) **Castel Sant'Angelo**
Lungotevere Castello; Tel: 6875036

*When the popes fell victim to politics and persecution, they took refuge in this drum-shaped fortress on the banks of the Tiber. Originally built by Hadrian in 135 AD as his personal mausoleum, the Castel Sant'Angelo was added to — layer upon layer — to function as fortress, prison and papal shelter (connected to the Vatican by raised rampart). Work your way up through history via the spiral ramp (which once led to Hadrian's burial chamber) to the Angel Courtyard (graced by an angel that stood atop the castle until the 18th century) to Alexander VI's Courtyard (with piles of ammo used in medieval times) to the elaborately frescoed papal apartments (where Pope Paul III and others dashed in times of trouble) to the Treasury (with six-foot tall lock box where the popes stashed their silver and secret records). The highlight is the amazing **view** from the **rooftop terrace** (also enjoy a drink at the rooftop cafe). Nearby **Ponte Sant'Angelo** is edged with ten angels sculpted by Bernini's studio (each angel bears an instrument of Christ's martyrdom). This was the Vatican's main approach until 1450 when, during a Jubilee celebration, 200 pilgrims were crushed to death on the bridge.*

Details: Daily, 9-2. Last entry one hour before closing. Cost: LL.

(28) **Piazza Navona**

*Thousands of tourists and natives come to see and be seen in Rome's grandest piazza, known as much for its street performers and sketch artists as for its Bernini fountains. Piazza Navona has always been the hub of public spectacle — even as far back as the 1st century when great athletic contests were held in Emperor Domitian's stadium that stood on this site (the stadium entrance door can still be seen in Piazza Tor Sanguigna). In the 15th century jousts were held here and, in the 18th century, the piazza was transformed into a shallow lake through which coaches of the nobility paraded. Thank Pope Innocent X for Piazza Navona's present look — he commissioned many of its landmarks in honor of his family, whose mansion stood at the southwest end (now the Brazilian embassy). The most famous of these landmarks, at the piazza's center, is the **Fountain of the Four Rivers**, designed in 1651 by Bernini (who won the commission by bribing the Pope's highly influential sister-in-law with a silver model of his proposed work). Its four figures represent the four largest rivers of the 17th century: the Danube, the Nile (whose veil indicates its unknown source), the Ganges and the Plate. The fountain is considered a masterpiece, though Bernini himself hated the outcome, once stating, "I am ashamed to have done so poorly." At the piazza's south end is the **Fountain of the Moor**, also by Bernini, and at the north end is the 19th-century **Fountain of Neptune**.*

Details: The piazza is great to stroll at night when lights illuminate the fountains.

(29) **Piazza della Pace**

*While vestiges of Rome's medieval past abound in the area around Piazza Navona, none are more alluring than this scenic piazza hidden in a labyrinth of winding, stone-paved streets. Dominating the piazza is **Santa Maria della Pace**, the repository of stunning art thanks to a steady stream of visitors who made this one of Rome's most popular churches in the 16th century. In addition to a wonderful Bramante-designed cloister (completed in 1504), you will discover Raphael's Sibyl frescoes (first chapel on right) and stuccoes by da Sangallo (second chapel on right; Vicolo Arco della Pace 5; under restoration). Just right, find the unmarked entrance to 16th-century **Santa Maria dell'Anima**, which gets rave reviews for a hidden courtyard filled with statues, plants, and stone urns (Via della Pace 20; daily, 7-7).*

Details: Viewed any time.

Legend

- 🔴 Historic Landmark
- 🟣 Best Museum
- 🟢 Superior Shopping
- 🟠 Hidden Treasure
- 🔴 Ancient Ruin
- ⚪ Also Good for Children
- **A** Metropolitana (Metro Line A)
- **B** Metropolitana (Metro Line B)
- **i** Tourist Information
- ▨ Steps

HELPFUL HINTS

GETTING AROUND

To and From Leonardo da Vinci International Airport (a.k.a. Fiumicino): a 30-minute express train runs from Fiumicino to Termini train station (in city center). Departures daily, 7:45 am-10 pm, every 30-60 minutes (cost: 13,000L). Taxis cost around 70,000L to get to the city center (use only officially licensed yellow or white cabs!).

In Rome: Rome is best seen on foot, with a pair of very sturdy shoes (the cobblestone streets can be murder in heels or sneakers). Taxis, though not cheap, are the most efficient way to get to your starting destination (and then hoof it from there). The bus/tram system is extensive, but complex and time-consuming. Purchase your ticket before boarding and time-stamp it on board; tickets are valid for 75 minutes of travel (cost: 1,500L; tickets sold at tobacco shops and some newsstands, as are detailed bus route maps). The Metro, with only two lines operating, is quite limited (cost: 1,500L). Daily and weekly passes for unlimited travel on bus/tram/metro are also available. The fearless can try out a scooter, and the not-so-fearless can stick to bikes (see annotation 53).

SPECIAL SUGGESTIONS

The following special suggestions will make your stay in Rome even more memorable:
- Contemplate early Christian Rome along peaceful Clivo di Scauro (see annotation 13).
- Wander the mazelike streets of the Jewish Ghetto (see annotation 18).
- Browse the antique shops of elegant Via Giulia and Via dei Coronari (see annotations 21 and 30).
- Spend time below St. Peter's in a fascinating necropolis guided tour (see annotation 24).
- Enjoy terrace views from Castel Sant'Angelo and San Pietro in Montorio (see annots. 27 and 63).
- Pay homage to artist Caravaggio at San Luigi dei Francesi (see annotation 32).
- Sip a cappuccino at the rooftop bar of the Hotel Eden (see annotation 47).
- Watch the sunset from the Pincio and then walk to the Spanish Steps (see annotation 48).
- Rent a bike to tour the Borghese Gardens (see annotation 53).
- Picnic amidst the orange trees of Parco Savello on the Aventine Hill (see annotation 60).

PAPAL AUDIENCES

The Pope holds a general audience weekly on **Wed. at 11 am** at Sala Nervi in Vatican City. Apply for free tickets several weeks in advance by writing to Prefettura della Casa Pontificia, Citta del Vaticano 00120 Roma, indicating the date you want to attend and your hotel. Or, upon arrival, get tickets at the Prefettura office (weekdays, 9-1; located in St. Peter's Square at end of the right colonnade where Swiss Guard is stationed; tel: 69883273). An easier way to see the Pope is on **Sun. at noon** when he appears at his study window in St. Peter's Square to bless the crowd.

SHOPPING

Stores are generally open Mon. to Sat., 9:30-1, 4-7:30 (some stay open continuously), and are usually closed Mon. morning from Sept. to June, and Sat. afternoons in July and Aug. Purchases in Rome are subject to a Value-Added Tax (VAT) which can be reclaimed if you spend more than 300,000 lire <u>in a single store.</u> To reclaim VAT: 1) get a Tax-free Cheque from store where you made purchases; 2) present cheque, together with purchases, at the airport Customs Office to get a stamp; 3) bring stamped cheque to the airport's Refund Desk to get instant cash (note that some stores participate in a tax-back scheme where cheque must be mailed to get refund).

GENERAL TIPS

Bring binoculars as some of Rome's best sights are on ceilings or atop columns. Don't wear sleeveless tops, shorts, or short skirts, as you won't be able to enter the city's many churches (most notably St. Peter's). To find out what's on, purchase the magazine *Roma c'è*, for a weekly listing of events in English or, if your Italian is good, get the Thurs. edition of *La Repubblica* for its supplement, *La Trova Roma*. Both are available at newsstands (cost: 1,500L).

QUICK TRIPS

NOT SHOWN ON MAP

MUSEUM OF ROMAN CIVILIZATION Piazza Agnelli 10; Tel: 5926135

Experience the history of Rome at this vast museum, located in the EUR suburb. Through reproductions, plaster casts and scale models (including a gigantic model of the city in the 4th century), you can see what the Roman forums, baths and aqueducts looked like before they fell to ruin.
The EUR was the brainchild of Mussolini, who conceived of six acres of Fascist monuments to
celebrate "all the sciences, arts and all forms of work and activity." The war put an abrupt end to
Mussolini's plans, and the area is now home to many government buildings.

Details: Tues. to Sat., 9-7, Sun., 9-1. Cost: L. Metro: Line B to EUR Fermi (15 minutes).

OSTIA ANTICA Viale dei Romagnoli 717; Tel: 5650022

If you can't make it to Pompeii head to Ostia, once the main commercial port of ancient Rome (with
100,000+ inhabitants), and now a fascinating ruin. The port silted up in the first two centuries and
Ostia was left a soggy swamp whose buildings were buried under sand and mud. Today, much has
been exhumed and the extensive remains of well-preserved baths, temples, warehouses, theatres
(where plays are still performed in summer), libraries, villas and shops give the visitor an intriguing
indication of Ostia's once-powerful position as the main nerve center of the Roman supply network.
Go on a sunny day to best appreciate the site.

Details: Daily, 9-5. Cost: LL. Metro: Line B to Magliana (15 minutes), then 20-minute train ride
to Ostia. Short walk from station to excavations.

TIVOLI

For over 2,000 years the wealthiest of Romans built their summer palaces around this town, the
remains of which can still be seen in two world renowned landmarks. The **Villa d'Este** (in Tivoli)
— the 16th-century retirement estate of Cardinal d'Este — is famous for its Renaissance gardens,
spread in terraces along the hillside. Featuring a profusion of whimsical fountains of every size and
shape, the gardens were a watery playground where the Cardinal lavishly entertained his distin-
guished guests. Just four miles southwest of town are the remains of Emperor Hadrian's private
retreat — **Hadrian's Villa** — built from 118 to 135 AD, and incorporating reproductions of favorite
monuments Hadrian discovered in his travels through Egypt and Greece. Hadrian spared no
expense on his personal comfort (entire valleys, complete with temples, were replicated!), building
baths, assembly halls, libraries, stadium and personal residence (all connected via underground
passage). The ruins are a remarkable tribute to ancient world architecture.

Details: Both Villa d'Este and Hadrian's Villa are open daily, 9-5. Cost for each: LL. Metro: Line
B to Rebibbia (15 minutes), then 45-minute COTRAL bus to Tivoli.

VIA APPIA ANTICA (APPIAN WAY)

Strewn with monumental tombs and indentations made by long-gone chariot wheels, the Appian
Way is one of the world's most historic thoroughfares. Begun in 312 BC by Roman Censor Appius
Claudius to connect Rome to southern Italy, the road is lined with the remains of funeral monuments and **catacombs** (multi-level underground cemeteries) dating to ancient times when
Roman law prohibited burials inside the city walls. The most picturesque stretch of road starts at
the **Tomb of Cecilia Metella** (a drum-shaped tomb built for a Roman noblewoman in 1 BC;
Tues. to Sat., 9-4, Sun. and Mon., 9-1). From here, majestic cypress trees give way to open coun-
tryside, dotted with ruins (walk two miles to Via Tor Carbone). More accessible landmarks are closer to the road's start, like the **Catacombs of San Callisto** (Rome's first Christian cemetery; tours
Thurs. to Tues., 8:30-12, 2:30-5; Cost: LL) and adjacent **Catacombs of San Sebastiano** (which
once housed the bodies of Sts. Peter and Paul; tours Fri. to Wed., 8:30-12, 2:30-5; Cost: LL).

Details: Bus 218 goes from Piazza di San Giovanni in Laterano to the Catacombs of San Callisto
(15 minutes).

30 **Via dei Coronari**

Pretty Via dei Coronari gets its name from the rosarymakers ("coronari") whose shops once supplied the vast number of visitors making a Vatican pilgrimage. Today, antique stores have replaced the religious trinket shops, and buyers and browsers will find the street a treasure trove of high-end goodies. In May and mid-Oct. the dealer's association rolls out the red carpet on its sidewalks to host an antiques fair. Even if you aren't in the market, don't miss a visit.

Details: For store hours see "Shopping" on the Helpful Hints page.

31 **Via dell'Orso**

Few streets better capture the flavor of medieval Rome than tiny Via dell'Orso. This ancient alley once hosted the likes of Rabelais, Montaigne and Goethe, all of whom bedded down at the famous **Hostaria dell'Orso** *— the oldest inn in town — which catered to visiting Vatican dignitaries from the 15th to 18th-centuries (the inn still stands and is now a restaurant/nightclub). Today, the surrounding jumble of narrow streets contain some of Rome's most intriguing museums including:* **Museo Napoleonico** *(with mementos from Napoleon's family, many of whom lived in Rome; Via Zanardelli 1; Tues. to Sat., 9-7, Sun., 9-1; closed Aug.; Cost: L),* **Museo Praz** *(displaying art critic Mario Praz's 1,400+ pieces of 18th-century antique furniture, paintings, and engravings; also at Via Zanardelli 1; guided tours on the hour, Mon., 2:30-6:30, Tues. to Sun., 9-1, 2:30-6:30; Cost: L; Reserve; tel: 6861089), and 15th-century* **Palazzo Altemps** *(brilliantly restored and containing a very important Greek and Roman antiquity collection; Via Sant'Apollinare 8; Tues. to Sun., 10-5; Cost: LL; tel: 6833759).*

Details: Viewed any time.

32 **San Luigi dei Francesi**
Via Santa Giovanna d'Arco; Tel: 688271

Caravaggio (1571-1610), one of the seminal painters of the Renaissance, left his greatest legacy at the French national church, a glorious stop just steps from Piazza Navona. In the last chapel on the left are three of the artist's finest works (right to left): the Martyrdom of St. Matthew, St. Matthew and the Angel, *and* The Calling of St. Matthew. *Though his paintings were legendary (powerfully realistic images enhanced by strong contrasts between light and shadow), Caravaggio achieved even greater fame because his art sparked so much controversy. He depicted religious characters as ordinary people — modeling them on the undesirables he befriended — and the trio you see here were initially rejected by priests who thought Caravaggio disrespectful of his subject (St. Matthew is portrayed with dirty feet!). Ultimately, their greatness was recognized and the paintings stayed (though the tempestuous Caravaggio himself was forced to leave Rome after murdering a man during a tennis match). Caravaggio fans should also detour to nearby* **Sant'Agostino** *where you will be rewarded with* Madonna dei Pellegrini, *in which the artist's prostitute girlfriend posed as the Virgin Mary (first chapel on left; intersection of Via Agostino and Via Scrofa; daily, 7:45-12, 4:30-7:30).*

Details: Daily, 7:30-12:30, 3:30-7. Closed Thurs. afternoon.

33 **Sant'Andrea della Valle**
Piazza Sant'Andrea della Valle; Tel: 6861339

Richly decorated with rare marble and some of Rome's great frescoes, Sant'Andrea della Valle is not an itinerary choice, it's a must! The great geniuses of the 17th century had a hand in its design, including Maderno (who built the dome, second in size to St. Peters), Lanfranco (who painted the dome's frescoes using a trompe l'oeil technique later copied in church domes worldwide), and Domenichino (who painted the apse with intricate scenes from the life of St. Andrew). Go on a sunny day, when the filtering light casts a golden glow over the apse. Just east, at **Area Sacra**, *four ancient temples sit serenely amidst chaotic traffic, and just west, the small* **Museo Barracco** *houses 400+ antiquities from Egypt, Greece and Rome (Corso Vittorio Emanuele II 168; Tues. to Sat., 9-7, Sun., 9-1; Cost: L).*

Details: Daily, 7:30-12, 4:30-7.

Via dei Cestari

Don't be surprised by the nuns, bishops and cardinals that stroll this street, for this is the heart of religious supply stores and <u>the</u> place to check out the finest in cassocks or cardinal's socks. At street's end, discover the official papal haberdasher, Gammarelli, who swathes the new pope in papal white (Via Santa Chiara 34).

Details: For store hours see "Shopping" on the Helpful Hints page.

Santa Maria sopra Minerva
Piazza della Minerva 42; Tel: 6793926

Rome's churches are also its best museums, and few boast as many outstanding works of art as Santa Maria sopra Minerva. An "around-the-altar" tour will lead to Michelangelo's sculpture of Christ carrying the Cross (the bronze "loincloth" was added later; left of altar), and superb frescoes by Botticelli's mentor, Filippo Lippi (last chapel on right; be sure to turn on the chapel light box). Noted (and notorious) Italians fill the delicately sculpted tombs throughout the church, including: St. Catherine of Siena (who persuaded the popes to return to Rome after they abandoned the city in 1309 for a palace in Avignon; under altar), the 16th-century Medici Popes, Leo X and Clement VII (who looted the church treasury; behind altar), and Pope Paul IV (who locked the Jews into the ghetto; second chapel on right). The church dates to the 13th century (though it was rebuilt in the Gothic style) and gets its name from the ruins of Minerva's temple over which it is built. In its **piazza**, *Bernini designed the whimsical marble elephant with obelisk mounted on its back in tribute to Pope Alexander VII, who thought the elephant a symbol of wisdom. For a great* **view** *of the Pantheon dome and other landmarks, take the elevator to the Holiday Inn* **roof terrace** *(south end of the piazza).*

Details: Daily, 7-12, 4-7.

Pantheon
Piazza della Rotonda; Tel: 68300230

Some of the world's greatest domed buildings — London's St. Paul's Cathedral, Washington, D.C.'s Capitol Building, and even Rome's St. Peter's — all have Emperor Hadrian to thank for providing an astonishing architectural landmark as a model. Amazingly, the Pantheon survives almost wholly intact from when Hadrian built this temple "to all the gods" between 118 and 125 AD (over the site of a temple built by Marcus Agrippa in 27 BC; the inscription to Marcus Agrippa over the portico was actually placed there by Hadrian). The Pantheon's perfectly proportioned dome — wider than St. Peter's and supported without columns or buttresses — reflects Hadrian's design genius (part of the trick was to use lighter material as the dome rises to the summit). The oculus (the 30-foot round opening in the roof dubbed the "eye of God") is the only source of light, and the Pantheon's seven recesses were once ringed with seven statues of gods dripping with jewels. Though the bronze doors are original, the bronze ceiling tiles didn't fare as well — Pope Urban VIII stole them to give Bernini the material to cast the

Vatican's Baldacchino. The Pantheon was converted into a Christian church in 609, a fortress in the 12th century and a bullfight arena in the 17th century. Today, it houses the tombs of artist Raphael and two Italian kings (Vittorio Emanuele and Umberto).

Details: Mon. to Sat., 9-6:30, Sun., 9-1. Cost: Free.

 ### Sant'Ignazio di Loyola
Piazza di Sant'Ignazio; Tel: 6794406

Definitely enter "stage right" through the beautiful ochre and yellow buildings that surround the magical **Piazza di Sant'Ignazio**, designed by Filippo Raguzzini in 1728 to look like an opera set. At center "spotlight" is this 17th-century church, home to a masterpiece of optical illusion — a frescoed ceiling featuring St. Ignatius's entry into paradise. Though the figures appear to surge toward the heavens, the ceiling is actually flat, a sleight of hand that is the work of celebrated artist Andrea Pozzo (1642-1709) whose design took into account the lack of funds available to actually build a dome. A yellow marble disk in the center of the nave shows you the ideal viewing spot. The church prides itself on its acoustics and hosts musical events throughout the year (tel: 6865704 for schedule information). Just north, along Vicolo Burro, discover peaceful **Piazza di Petra**, where Rome's Stock Exchange (Borsa) occupies a colonnaded 2nd-century temple that once honored Hadrian (not open to the public).

Details: Daily, 7:30-12:30, 4-7:15.

 ### Column of Marcus Aurelius
Piazza Colonna

The most profoundly intellectual of the emperors, Marcus Aurelius (161-180 AD) presided over a vast domain beset by incessant warfare, disease and financial hardship. With the Empire rapidly disintegrating, no wonder Aurelius looks so sad in the sculpted reliefs of this 100-foot marble newsreel, dedicated in 193 AD to chronicle his victorious campaigns. A statue of Aurelius capped the column until 1589 when it was replaced with the current tribute to St. Paul. On the piazza's north side are the Prime Minister's offices, housed in 17th-century **Palazzo Chigi**, and west of the piazza is 17th-century **Palazzo di Montecitorio**, home to the Italian Chamber of Deputies (built on the site of the crematorium that once reduced Emperors to ashes; Piazza de Montecitorio).

Details: Viewed any time.

 ### Palazzo Doria Pamphilj
Enter at Piazza del Collegio Romano 2; Tel: 6797323

For a glimpse of the luxurious lifestyle of Italian nobility, step inside this magnificent recently restored 15th-century palazzo — ancestral home of the Pamphilj clan. While the setting is to be admired, the artwork is to be savored — numerous galleries are filled with an impressive family collection of 15th to 18th-century Italian masters, including works by Caravaggio, Titian and Carracci. The highlight is Velázquez's celebrated portrait of Pope Innocent X Pamphilj (the Pope's sad-looking features accurately depict his sorry plight — his family stole all his valuables while he was on his deathbed and then stuck him into an ill-fitting coffin in the Vatican!). Don't miss the lavishly decorated **private apartments** which include a winter garden, ballroom, salon and private chapel. Family members still live in several of the palace's 400+ rooms.

Details: Fri. to Wed., 10-5. Cost: LL. Private apts.: tour at 11 and 12. Cost: LL.

Il Gesù
Piazza del Gesù; Tel: 6786343

One visit to jewel-encrusted Il Gesù and you'll know why it ranks with St. Peter's as one of Rome's most beautiful ecclesiastical landmarks. Commissioned in 1568 as the main church of the Jesuits — an order founded by St. Ignatius of Loyola in the mid 1500s to counter the growing Protestant movement — Il Gesù was designed to let the "word of God be more easily heard" (notice the broad nave built to get the congregation more involved). As the papacy's strength solidified in the 1600s, Il Gesù became more and more elaborate, and over the course of the next two centuries it was richly decorated with precious stones and frescoes. Highlights include: a frescoed dome and nave by Baciccia (featuring Old Testament figures in flight), and St. Ignatius's altar designed by 17th-century artist Andrea Pozzo (angels above the statue allegedly hold the world's largest piece of lapis lazuli while St. Ignatius's remains rest in an urn below). Adjacent to the church are St. Ignatius's private rooms, with a trompe l'oeil corridor also by Pozzo (Piazza del Gesù 45).

Details: Daily, 9-12, 4-7:15.

 ## Piazza Venezia

*Crowning Piazza Venezia is the hard-to-miss **Vittorio Emanuele Monument**, derisively called the "Wedding Cake" for its stark white layers. Inaugurated in 1911, the monument honors the king who unified Italy in 1870 and anointed Rome the capital (up to then, Italy was a decentralized collection of small duchies and states). This incongruous landmark — so massive that its designer died of exhaustion during its construction — dwarfs even the most egotistical of monuments built by the emperors. At the piazza's eastern edge is the out-matched 15th-century **Palazzo Venezia**, once a papal residence and later the headquarters of Fascist leader Benito Mussolini. From its balcony, Mussolini whipped the masses into a frenzy, while inside his office (the Sala dei Mappamundo), visitors had to walk a full 60 feet before Il Duce would even take notice! Today, the palazzo is a far more relaxed setting in which one finds special exhibits (in the Sala dei Mappamundo) and a rarely visited **decorative arts museum** (with an excellent collection of ceramics, tapestries and more).*

Details: Museum: Tues. to Sat., 9-2, Sun., 9-1. Last entry 30 minutes before closing. Cost: LL. Special Exhibits Cost: LLL. Enter museum at Via del Plebiscito 118.

 ## Palazzo Colonna
Via della Pilotta 17; Tel: 6794362

*For an off-the-beaten path experience that even most natives have yet to discover, visit the Palazzo Colonna, home to one of the world's most majestic "living rooms." The residence of the Colonna family (whose heirs include one Pope, 30 cardinals and numerous statesmen), the palazzo is the work of the two most famous Colonna descendants — Pope Martin V commissioned it in 1417 and Cardinal Girolamo Colonna renovated the palazzo in the 17th century, adding the unbelievable 10,000-foot **Grand Salon**. Yellow marble columns (imported from Africa), a massive frescoed ceiling (representing episodes in the life of Colonna family members), and rare artwork (with paintings by Poussin, Lanfranco, Rubens and others) form a setting that makes the salon a star attraction. Also viewable is the Hall of Desks (earning its name from the cabinet covered with carved ivory reproductions of Michelangelo's works) and Martin V's Throne Room (kept ready by the family in case their famous relative paid a visit). Those who make an even closer inspection will find a cannonball embedded in the salon's stairs, a souvenir from a battle with the French in 1849.*

Details: Sat., 9-1. Closed Aug. Cost: LL.

Trevi Fountain
Piazza di Trevi

Enhance your chances of a return trip to Rome by performing the famous "over-the-left-shoulder Trevi coin toss" (a tradition welcomed by the Italian government who makes sure the lire stay put in the city treasury, while foreign currencies are donated to the Red Cross!). Tucked into narrow backstreets, the city's largest fountain readily reflects designer Nicola Salvi's thirty years of hard labor (1732-1762). Giant stone gods (Neptune, flanked by Abundance on the left, and Health on the right) and prancing horses frolic daily in the city's cleanest water. Twin reliefs below the cornice tell the story of the Trevi's origins which date to 19 BC when Augustus's right-hand man, Agrippa, built an aqueduct that still supplies the Trevi's water. The right image depicts a young maiden pointing out the source of the water to Agrippa's soldiers, and the left shows Agrippa approving the aqueduct. Opposite the fountain is **Santi Vincenzo e Anastasio**, the popes' parish church when they resided at nearby Palazzo del Quirinale (the hearts of 22 pontiffs are stored in the apse walls; daily, 8:30-12, 4-6:30). Just north, the **Accademia di San Luca**, a training ground for Renaissance up-and-comers, displays works donated as a prerequisite to membership (Via Stamperia; Mon., Wed., Fri., 10-12:30; closed summer). Across the street, the **Calcografia**'s engraving collection is one of the world's largest (Mon. to Sat., 9-1, Sun., 10-1; small display on ground floor).

Details: Viewed any time, but the fountain is particularly stunning at night when it is lit up.

Palazzo del Quirinale
Piazza del Quirinale; Tel: 46991

The palace of popes and presidents, the Palazzo del Quirinale was long the private domain of a privileged few. Begun in 1573 by Pope Gregory XIII and finally completed by Pope Clement XII in 1740, the Quirinale was the papal "Camp David," whose hilltop setting was the coolest spot in town when Roman summers were too much to bear at the Vatican. In 1870 the Italian kings moved in, and since 1946 the palace has been the official residence of Italy's President. In 1994, the Quirinale opened its doors to the public to show off the art treasures amassed by its famous residents, among them a rare collection of frescoes, and Renaissance and Baroque furnishings. Via **guided tour** you'll view a variety of exquisite galleries decorated by a succession of popes and, after your tour, enjoy an unrivaled city view.

Details: Guided tours: second and fourth Sun. of each month, 8:30-12:30. Passport required for admission. Reservation not required. Cost: Free.

Sant'Andrea al Quirinale
Via del Quirinale 29; Tel: 48903187

Just up the street from Palazzo del Quirinale are two small churches with great artistic legacies. Bernini designed **Sant'Andrea al Quirinale** in 1658, calling it "his greatest accomplishment" — high praise from a man who designed the piazza in front of St. Peter's! A clever mix of curves and countercurves gives this small space a sense of majesty, and the pink marble interior earned it the nickname the "Pearl of the Baroque." A few yards away is **San Carlo alle Quattro Fontane**, designed in 1634 by Borromini, who masterfully fitted the church into an irregular wedge-shaped plot of land. The breathtaking architecture and elaborate interior sculpture form a jewel that has few equals (Via del Quirinale 23; daily, 9:30-12:30, 4-6; closed Sat. afternoon). In each of the four corners of the adjacent intersection is a 16th-century fountain — **Quattro Fontane** — where two stone males (river gods) and two stone females (symbolizing strength and fidelity), relax in oblivious splendor to passing traffic.

Details: Wed. to Mon., 8-12, 4-7. Closed Aug.

Palazzo Barberini
Via delle Quattro Fontane 13; Tel: 4814591

A treasure trove of 13th to 18th-century paintings awaits your inspection at the Palazzo Barberini — built by the powerful Barberini family in 1627 and, today, the home of the **Galleria Nazionale d'Arte Antica**. *On display are important private holdings of the Barberinis and additional donations from other wealthy Italian families. Highlights include: Holbein's* Portrait of Henry VIII *(painted the day Henry married Anne of Cleves) and* La Fornarina *(a portrait of Raphael's mistress). The palazzo's "jewel in the crown" is its Grand Salon, with the largest ceiling fresco ever painted for a non-church, created by Pietro da Cortona from 1632 to 1639 (note the bees — symbols of the Barberini family — swarming in the middle). Unfortunately, a large part of the palazzo is being restored and the Barberini private apartments are no longer open. Pay a quick visit to one of our favorite fountains — the water-spouting Triton — designed by Bernini in the 17th century and still holding court in* **Piazza Barberini**.

Details: Tues. to Sat., 9-6, Sun., 9-1. Last entry 30 minutes before closing. Cost: LL.

Via Veneto

Though the fabled "Vee-Vee" is no longer the haunt of paparazzi and playboys, this stately boulevard — laced with grand hotels — is definitely worth a stroll. At its southern end, take in the bizarre **Santa Maria della Concezione**, *whose basement is decorated with the skulls and bones of 4,000 Capuchin monks buried here between 1528 and 1870 (Via Veneto 27; daily, 9-12, 3-6). At its midpoint, note the grand* **American Embassy** *(at the intersection of Via Liguria), and just off the northern end, visit the Hotel Eden* **rooftop bar** *for an incredible* **view** *of the dome of St. Peter's and a piano player tickling the ivories (one of our favorite stops in Rome; Via Ludovisi 49).*

Details: Viewed any time.

The Spanish Steps

Pastel-colored palazzos and swaying palm trees provide a bewitching frame to what is arguably the world's most romantic landmark — the 137 white marble steps that cascade down from Trinità dei Monti church to Piazza di Spagna. The Spanish Steps, picture-postcard perfect anytime, reach a photogenic peak in April and May when blanketed with azaleas (and covered with the youth of the world, who come by the hordes despite a 1995 seven month restoration prompting new regulations forbidding eating, drinking, or sleeping). Completed in 1726, the steps earned their name from the Spanish Embassy which set up shop in the piazza in the early 17th century. But, ironically, it was the French who actually paid for the steps' construction in an effort to create a grand approach to the French-owned **Trinità dei Monti**, *still located at the steps' top (daily, 9:30-12, 4-6). At the bottom, in the* **Piazza di Spagna**, *is the enchanting* **Fontana della Barcaccia** *("leaking boat" fountain, executed in 1629 by Bernini's father, Pietro, in memory of the flood of 1598), and the* **Keats-Shelley Memorial House** *(where Keats lived from 1820 to his death in 1821, and where bizarre items like death masks and hair follicles are displayed alongside first editions; Mon. to Fri., 9-1, Sat., 2:30-5:30; Cost: LL). Detour west, from the top of the steps, to 16th-century* **Villa Medici**. *Home to the French Academy, the villa is renowned for its garden with original Renaissance layout still intact (garden visited via one hour guided tour: mid Apr.-end June, Sun. only; tour leaves every half hour from 10-12:30; Cost: L; call first to confirm hours; tel: 67611).*

Details: Viewed any time.

49 **Via Condotti and environs**

Zig and zag your way through a who's who of designer names at Rome's premiere shopping district, located at the foot of the Spanish Steps (and bounded by Piazza di Spagna, Via del Corso, Via Frattina and Via Vittoria). If your lire are limitless, then enter the boutiques and ateliers of the fashion famous scattered about the area. The most celebrated of the streets is Via Condotti, and an afternoon's wander can find you with scarves from Gucci (Via Condotti 8), luggage from Vuitton (No. 11), bags from Beltrami (No. 84) and shoes from Ferragamo (No. 74). But also pay special attention to the parallel streets like **Via Borgognona** *(to uncover Ferre at No. 6 and Fendi at No. 36-40), and smaller perpendicular streets like* **Via Bocca di Leone** *(to find Versace). Bring an extra suitcase … and an extra credit card!*

Details: For store hours see "Shopping" on the Helpful Hints page.

50 **Via Margutta**

The highest of the high-end antique and gallery shopping can be found on Via Margutta (a.k.a. "Street of the Artists"). And though you may not be able to afford the museum-quality pieces (with price tags to match), you will appreciate the beauty of this elegant, cobbled thoroughfare. The street has always been the haunt of creative types (Federico Fellini lived at No. 113 until his death in 1994), and is best experienced in June and Oct. when the street association hosts its art fairs. While its neighbor, **Via del Babuino***, may be more highly trafficked (and is also good to stroll), we prefer this upscale oasis and highly recommend a stop.*

Details: For store hours see "Shopping" on the Helpful Hints page.

51 **Altar of Peace (Ara Pacis)**
Via di Ripetta

Emperor Augustus commissioned this magnificent white marble altar in 13 BC as a celebration of peace throughout the Roman Empire. Protected today by a glass enclosure, the altar is richly decorated with some of ancient Rome's finest sculpture, most notably reliefs of those who attended the altar's dedication ceremony. The altar's east side shows Augustus and his family (Augustus is the one cut in half), and the west side features a procession of priests and magistrates. Detailed acanthus leaves adorn the altar's four lower panels, and mythological scenes are sculpted into the upper panels around the doors. Incredibly, the altar was patched together in the 20th century as, bit by bit, pieces were discovered in many of Europe's major museums. Just east is the **Mausoleum of Augustus***, a crumbling cylinder that saw much grander days when Augustus built it in 28 BC as his final resting place (not open). A small* **antique print market** *operates at nearby Piazza Borghese (Mon. to Sat. mornings).*

Details: Tues. to Sat., 9-5, Sun., 9-1. Cost: L.

52 **Piazza del Popolo**

For centuries, the Piazza del Popolo — Rome's majestic "front door" — welcomed a host of recognized figures through its 16th-century gate, all of whom agreed that no other city had as fine an approach. Today, visitors are still awed by this theatrical oval at whose "center stage" rises a 79-foot-high **obelisk***, shipped from Egypt by Emperor Augustus for the Circus Maximus, and moved here in 1589. Twin churches, commissioned by Pope Alexander VII in 1660, dominate the piazza's south end (though they appear to be identical, they are actually different shapes). And at the piazza's north end is the 15th-century church of* **Santa Maria del Popolo***, containing an outstanding collection of art, courtesy of illustrious Italian families* who donated funds for its various private chapels. Inside you'll find two of Caravaggio's finest works (left of altar), frescoes by Pinturicchio (apse ceiling and first chapel on right), and a Raphael-designed chapel for banker Agostini Chigi (with mosaics of Chigi's astrological sign; second chapel on left; daily, 7-12:30, 4-7). The piazza was not just an entrance, but an exit as well – public executions were held here in the 18th and 19th centuries, and riderless horse races ran from here down the Via del Corso (a major artery today). Climb the steps at the piazza's northeast corner to the **Pincio Gardens** for one of the best **views** in Rome. At dusk, a golden glow hovers over major Roman landmarks.

Details: Viewed any time.

 ### Villa Borghese/Galleria Borghese

Thank Cardinal Scipione Borghese for Rome's grandest public park, **Villa Borghese**, laid out in the early 17th-century to compliment the large villa he built to escape the oppressive summer heat. Today, the park is the place where all of Rome comes to stroll and jog, and the villa houses the **Galleria Borghese**, the "queen of the world's private art collections" (the Cardinal was a tireless collector!). Open to view is a sculpture collection worthy of the Louvre, with a hit parade of marble heads and torsos (including a scandalous Canova of Napoleon's sister, Paulina, posed topless on a chaise lounge!). The paintings are equally remarkable, featuring precious works by Caravaggio and Titian. The frescoed rooms in which the pieces are displayed, after a recently completed 13 year restoration, are as astounding as the art itself (located at the park's eastern edge; June-Sept., Tues. to Sun., 9-7; Oct.-May, Tues. to Sat., 9-5, Sun., 9-1; Cost: LLL; Reservations are a must; call 84241607 to reserve tickets). In the park's northwest corner is the **Villa Giulia National Etruscan Museum**, once Pope Julius III's 16th-century retreat and now home to the world's greatest concentration of Etruscan art – a civilization that flourished when Rome was just a collection of little huts (Tues. to Sat., 9-7, Sun., 9-1; Cost: LL).

Details: You can tour the park by bike (rentals available at I Bike Rome, located in the Borghese underground parking lot, Sector 3, or at Via Veneto 156; daily; tel: 3225240; scooter rentals are also available).

 ### Palazzo Massimo (National Museum of Rome)
Piazza dei Cinquecento; Tel: 48903500

A recent addition to the Roman cultural scene, the Palazzo Massimo is the new home of the National Museum of Rome's celebrated antiquity collection. Orphaned during the renovation of its original home at the **Baths of Diocletian** (ancient Rome's largest baths, built from 298 to 305 AD), the collection has been parceled out to several palazzos around town (ultimately to be reunited in this 19th-century mansion). Unfortunately, only a small number of sparsely filled rooms of Greek and Roman antiquities are currently open to the public, and the cost of entry is quite high relative to the contents (though the museum intends to display more items in the coming years). If you're in the area, detour a few blocks northwest to small, 17th-century **Santa Maria della Vittoria**. There you will find a side chapel designed by Bernini in the form of a "stage set," depicting the moment when God sent his messenger to pierce the soul of St. Theresa with an arrow. The agony (or ecstasy) of St. Theresa is witnessed by Cornaro family members in the side "boxes" (fourth chapel on left; Via XX Settembre 17; daily, 7-12, 4:30-7).

Details: Tues. to Sat., 9-2, Sun., 9-1. Last entry one hour before closing. Cost: LLL (ticket also gets you into the garden courtyard of the Baths of Diocletian across the street).

Santa Maria Maggiore
Piazza di Santa Maria Maggiore; Tel: 483195

The chilly origins of this basilica — one of the four largest in Rome — date to 352 AD when, legend has it, the Virgin Mary instructed Pope Liberius to build a church on the spot where snow would fall. When Liberius witnessed a miraculous midsummer snowfall the next day, this basilica was born. Santa Maria Maggiore is the only Roman basilica which, despite alterations, preserves its original shape, and is noted for superb 5th century mosaics above the nave, apse and chancel depicting scenes from the Old Testament. Other highlights include the shimmering ceiling (allegedly made with the first gold brought from America by Columbus), the altar (where a marble Pope Pius IX kneels in prayer in front of fragments of Jesus' crib), the monumental tombs of Popes Sixtus V and Pius V (decorated with reliefs of events in their reign; right of altar), and the lavish Pauline Chapel (with tombs of Popes Clement VIII and Paul V; left of altar). Every Aug. 5, flower petals rain down on the interior to re-enact Liberius's snowfall.

Details: Daily, 7-6:45.

San Clemente
Via di San Giovanni in Laterano; Tel: 70451018

Descend deeper and deeper below ground to discover three layers of Roman history at San Clemente, one of the city's most unique churches. The 12th-century basilica at street level (noted for the "vine of life" apse mosaic) is built above a 4th-century basilica (with beautiful fragments of early Christian frescoes) which, in turn, is built over a 1st-century palazzo (with temple dedicated to Mithras; remains of the temple include the altar room, lined with benches upon which devotees reclined after the ritual meal, and the school room). San Clemente is well worth a detour before you reach the point of ecclesiastical overload!

Details: Mon. to Sat., 9-12:30, 3:30-6, Sun., 10-12:30, 3:30-6. Cost for lower level: L.

San Giovanni in Laterano
Piazza di San Giovanni in Laterano; Tel: 77207991

A statue of Constantine stands just to the left of his 4th-century creation, one of Rome's most important (and earliest) churches and still the city's official cathedral. Numerous fires and earthquakes left little of Constantine's original basilica, and the church's present appearance is the result of a 17th-century interior alteration by Borromini and an 18th-century exterior redesign by Alexander Galilei. Over 20 Popes had a hand in its decor — no doubt because they used to live next door at the Lateran Palace (before it burned down in 1309 and they were forced to drop anchor at the Vatican). Look for: original bronze entry doors from the Curia in the Forum (at entrance), 12 colossal marble statues of the Apostles (completed by seven different sculptors from 1703 to 1718), a chapel supported by four columns allegedly from the Temple of Jupiter (left of apse), the altar where the Pope says mass (containing the preserved heads of Saints Peter and Paul), and a 13th-century cloister (entered on left aisle).

Details: Daily, 7-6. Cost for cloister entry: L (also includes visit to small museum).

Scala Santa/Sancta Sanctorum
Piazza di San Giovanni in Laterano 14

These two holy icons — the only pre-fire remains of the early popes' residence at the old Lateran Palace — are so sacred that they literally bring the pious to their knees. The Scala Santa is the "Holy Staircase" from which Christ descended after his judgment of death in Pontius Pilate's Jerusalem palace. Constantine's mother, Helena, allegedly brought the stair-

case back to Rome in 326 AD, and today one can find the faithful climbing the 28 wood-covered steps on their knees in fervent prayer. Accessible at the top of the Holy Staircase is the Sancta Sanctorum ("Holy of Holies"), the popes' private chapel when they lived at the Lateran Palace (the Lateran, rebuilt in the 16th century, now houses Vatican administrative offices). Nearby, at Porta San Giovanni, see remains of the **Aurelian Wall**, begun in 270 AD as a defense against Germanic tribes, and once 12 miles long, with 18 gates and 371 towers.

Details: Daily, 6:15 am-12:15, 3-6:30 pm.

 ### Baths of Caracalla
Viale delle Terme di Caracalla; Tel: 5758626

To fully appreciate the size and scale of ancient Rome, take a walk around the ruins of one of the world's earliest health clubs — the Baths of Caracalla. Inaugurated by Emperor Caracalla in 216 AD, these baths covered 25 acres and were the largest in the city until the Baths of Diocletian were built. Much of the layout is still intact, and it is easy to imagine 1,600+ people taking a dip in the caldarium (hot bath), tepidarium (tepid bath) or frigidarium (cold bath), lounging in the gym, libraries and gardens, or partaking of more sinister pleasures. At their zenith, these impressive baths were covered with mosaics (large portions of which are still visible), and richly decorated with outstanding works of art. The baths were used until 507 AD when the barbarians stopped all aqueducts flowing into the city. Outdoor opera performances used to be held in the caldarium in summer, but due to stress on the ruins the events were cancelled (though they may start up again, so call to confirm).

Details: Tues. to Sat., 9-5:30, Sun., Mon., 9-1. Last entry one hour before closing. Cost: LL. Note: the Baths of Caracalla are located in an area just southeast of dot on map.

 ### Aventine Hill

We definitely suggest a stroll on the Aventine Hill — a peaceful oasis of luxurious villas, ancient churches and atmospheric gardens that earns our highest marks for scenery and charm. Originally a haunt of merchants who traded on the Tiber, the hill is now an exclusive residential neighborhood whose lovely mansions give way to even lovelier scenery. In the 5th century a priest chose this site for a beautiful basilica, **Santa Sabina**, which still dominates the hill and is noted for its original wood doors carved with Old and New Testament scenes (Via Santa Sabina; daily, 7-12:30, 3:30-7). To the right and left of the church are two small **parks**, among the most serene spots in Rome (the larger is the **Parco Savello**). Both offer a canopy of orange trees, the peaceful sounds of trickling fountains and exceptional **views** of St. Peter's. Just a few yards south, near **Sant'Alessio**, peer through the entry keyhole of the **Villa of the Knights of Malta** to zoom in on St. Peter's dome in the distance (Piazza dei Cavalieri di Malta 3; villa not open to the public). Across the piazza, at pretty **Sant'Anselmo**, hear Gregorian chants on Sun. at 9:30 a.m. and then revive yourself with a cappuccino in the Hotel Sant'Anselmo courtyard. End your trek at the city's **rose garden** (off Clivo dei Publicii).

Details: Allow three hours to explore. Take Via Clivo dei Publicii and then Via Santa Sabina.

 ### Trastevere

If out-of-the-way corners and labyrinthine backstreets are what you're after, then head to the medieval quarter of Trastevere ("across the Tiber"). Once the home of "workers, foreigners and seafarers," Trastevere is now a haven for more elite clientele who delight in its tiny piazzas, intimate trattorias and winding, cobbled streets. To help you discover the neighborhood's varied charms we have created this **suggested walking route**: From **Tiber Island** (a heal-

*ing center since 293 BC; today a hospital still dominates most of the tiny island), cross the street to Piazza Piscinula. Follow Via Piscinula to the end and take a left on Via dei Salumi. In a few yards, take a right on Via dei Vascelari (to find 9th-century **Santa Cecilia**, built atop the tomb of St. Cecilia, whose death sentence included suffocation in her own hot baths and a botched decapitation; in the altar is a statue of the saint as she looked when her tomb was opened in 1599; daily, 10-12, 4-6). Go right on Via Madonna dell'Orto, and then left on Via Anicia to discover **San Francesco a Ripa** (containing Bernini's famous statue of Beata Ludovica Albertoni in "divine ecstasy"; last chapel on left; Mon. to Sat., 7-1, 4-7:30, Sun., 7-12, 4-7). Walk northwest on Via San Francesco a Ripa to **Piazza Santa Maria in Trastevere** (the heart of the district), and visit the **church** of the same name (known for outstanding apse and facade mosaics; daily, 7:30-12:30, 4-7). Take Via Paglia to Piazza Sant'Egidio (with small folklore **museum**; Tues. to Sat., 9-6:30, Sun., 9-12:30; Cost: L). Follow Via della Scala through the ancient city wall to Villa Farnesina and Palazzo Corsini (see annotation 62).*

Details: Allow four to five hours to leisurely cover the suggested walking route.

62 Villa Farnesina/Palazzo Corsini
Via della Lungara 230; Tel: 68801767/Via della Lungara 10; Tel: 68802323

*View the best of the Italian art world — without crowds or long lines — at our favorite face-to-face palazzos. Agostino Chigi, zillionaire banker to the popes, called upon the greatest artists of the early 16th century to decorate his lavish residence, **Villa Farnesina**. Chigi's triumph contains some of Rome's finest frescoes, most notably those painted by Raphael, who accepted the commission when Chigi invited Raphael's mistress to the villa for an extended stay. The villa was sold to the Farnese family in 1577 and it is now the property of the Italian government. Just across the street is the underrated 18th-century **Palazzo Corsini**, once the deluxe home of Queen Christina of Sweden and now a museum filled with noteworthy paintings by 17th and 18th-century artists like Reni, Rubens and Van Dyck. The palazzo's "backyard," one of Rome's prettiest patches of green, is the site of the University of Rome's **botanical garden (Orto Botanico)** — a 30-acre park with 7,000+ plant species. Have a seat by the serene fountain near the entrance and enjoy the tropical view (Mon. to Sat., 9-5:30; Cost: L).*

Details: Farnesina: Mon. to Sat., 9-1. Call first to confirm. Cost: Free. Corsini: Tues. to Fri., 9-7, Sat., 9-4, Sun, 9-1. Last entry 30 minutes before closing. Cost: LL.

63 Janiculum Hill

*Atop this hill one could find Julius Caesar inspecting his vineyards, or visiting his lover, Cleopatra, who was stashed in a villa nearby (she couldn't stay in Rome proper because Caesar's wife was there!). Today, Janiculum Hill is best known for the scenic **view** from its summit — **Piazza Garibaldi** — reached by walking up steep Via Garibaldi and even steeper Passeggiata Gianicolo. For a less strenuous hike (and less crowded panorama), stop at 15th-century **San Pietro in Montorio**. From the church's terrace, take in the sweep of the city and, in its courtyard, note the tiny, circular chapel known as the **Tempietto**, completed by Bramante in 1502. Built over the alleged spot where St. Peter was crucified, the Tempietto is considered the jewel of the Renaissance. When Pope Julius II saw it he immediately chose Bramante to redesign St. Peter's (access by steps at Via S. Pietro in Montorio off Via Garibaldi; Tues. to Sat., 9:30-12, 4:30-6:30, Sun., 9:30-12).*

Details: Viewed any time.